To help you
create a simpler,
more satisfying life,
improving
your mental and
physical well-being.

By Susie Bush-Ramsey

The purpose of the words that follow are to inspire. Included are hints, tips, and points to consider, along with actions that can be taken to prompt change.

This book is not intended to be a comprehensive guide, but an overview of 7 interconnected elements, which, when synchronized, can create a path for life to flow freely.

Steps to flow:

1 Breathe fully 9

2 Quieten my mind 21

3 Rise above my
emotions 51

4 Use my words
powerfully 73

5 Be thankful & kind........ 89

6 Minimalise my
materialism..................... 105

7 Refuel & exercise
purposefully.................... 121

Breathe fully

(Breathing)

Breathing fully
reduces stress,
boosts my
immune system,
and helps every
aspect of my body.

Pausing to notice
my breathing
periodically each day
is invaluable.

Breathe in
(mouth closed)
for as long as comfortable
Belly expands

– Pause –

Breathe out
(through the mouth)
for as long as comfortable
Belly contracts

My lungs can expand
fully as I breathe in,
my belly, chest and
ribs then rise like
an ocean wave.

When I exhale softly,
my lungs deflate and
my chest, ribs and
belly recede, just like
an ocean wave falls
to the sea-shore.

I can
consider:

- lying on my back with
  one hand on my chest
  and the other on my belly
  to notice how fully I'm breathing;

- taking 10 full breaths before
  going to sleep each night
  and when I first wake up
  each morning.

I can commit to:

- considering my posture throughout each day to help open up my chest.

- noticing my breathing and taking deep breaths each time I'm running water. For example when washing my hands or taking a shower.

A simple story...

At the age of 41 I was forced to pause unexpectedly and I realised that I had been in constant flight mode, too busy to even breathe properly. In fact, before this time, despite being a former athlete, I never even stopped to notice my breathing. When I did, I realised just how shallow it was. After only a week of pausing throughout the day to notice it, then inhaling and exhaling fully at least 10 times before going to sleep at night, I noticed a substantial difference to my overall well-being.

A scientific perspective:

When you breathe deeply, the air coming in through your nose fully fills your lungs, and you will notice that your lower belly rises. The ability to breathe so deeply and powerfully is not limited to a select few. This skill is inborn but often lies dormant. Reawakening it allows you to tap into one of your body's strongest self-healing mechanisms.

Source: Excerpt from 'Take a deep breath, Harvard Health'
https://www.health.harvard.edu/staying-healthy/take-a-deep-breath

An inspiring quote:

" Breathe. Let go.
And remind yourself that
this very moment is the
only one you know you
have for sure. "

Oprah Winfrey

Challenge 1

Before going to sleep at night take 10 full, deep breaths. Breathe in through your nose (for as long as comfortable). Pause. Breathe out through your mouth (for as long as comfortable). Give your full attention to the sensation of breathing to help quieten your mind as you drift off to sleep.

Quieten my mind

(Thinking)

My mind is an incredible tool that I can use to learn. Each time I learn or practise something, my mind gets stronger.

In the same way, negative thoughts get stronger if I consistently think about them.

The more I believe
negative thoughts,
the more defined
the pathways in my
brain become.

My brain has the ability to adapt and change.

Regardless of my genes,
childhood or past,
if I start thinking
differently, new pathways
can be established
and old, previously
well travelled ones
can fade away.

The negative voice
or thoughts I hear inside
my head, are not who
I am. My sense of worth
should not be derived
from them.

I could choose to stand back and see my negative thoughts as the voice of a person who is not me.

Viewing my thoughts from this perspective can cause them to subside as I stop taking ownership of them.

If my thoughts
are about my past
(things I can not change)
or my future
(things I can not
yet determine),
I waste valuable energy.

I can note down the
things I can control,
and then focus on
what is present.

I could consider my
thoughts like clouds –
If I allow them to fill my
mind and get too heavy,
they risk becoming a
storm in the form of
my emotions.

An Illustration

The sun
is always
present
even though
it may not
be visible

Lightning
Wind
Rain

Clouds

My Heart

My Spirit
Who I really am
My true value

Love, joy and peace

....

My Body

My emotions
Stress, fear, pain, envy

....

My Mind/Thoughts

My past and future

....

It is possible to
quieten my mind
by taking notice
of my breathing and
the present moment
– the things I see
and hear.

By focusing on the
present moment
(the things I can control),
I am able to reach beyond
the clouds and any storm
and begin living a
more peaceful life.

Taking notice of the present moment for what it is, and not judging it based on my previous experiences or future expectations, can bring a stillness to my mind.

If I flow with whatever life brings, then I can live in a place of peace.

Flowing with life and accepting the present moment for what it is, doesn't mean that you don't want change and can not plan and prepare accordingly.

I can consider how nature
adapts with the weather
and flows with the seasons.

The branches of a tree sway beautifully
with the wind. If they didn't move with
the wind, they would snap and break.

I can consider:

- experimenting with ways to manage my thoughts to allow my mind to quieten as often as possible.

  For example: thinking of any negative thoughts / voice as another person: or like clouds, and watching them pass by: or by labelling a repeating negative thought with a name to help identify patterns.

I can commit to:

- not taking negative thoughts on as my identity;

- thinking more about the present moment,

  (whilst being conscious not to think about this moment based on past experiences or future expectations).

A scientific perspective:

Neuroplasticity refers to your brain's ability to reorganize itself physically and functionally.

It is possible to improve and control your behaviour, thinking, and emotions.

Neurons that are used frequently develop stronger connections, and those that are not eventually die.

By developing new connections and pruning away weak ones, the brain is able to adapt.

https://www.health.harvard.edu/mind-and-mood/in-praise-of-gratitude

An inspiring quote:

"The primary cause of unhappiness is never the situation, but thought about it. Be aware of the thoughts you are thinking."

Eckhart Tolle

The Power of Now: A Guide to Spiritual Enlightenment

Having plans and hopes for the future can make me feel energised for tomorrow while still appreciating everyday life and enjoying the journey.

I can consider:

- What inspires me?

- What qualities do I have that could help others?

- What do I love doing the most?

- What do I value?

- What am I good at or
  what would I like to become
  good at?

- What would I like to learn,
  see and experience?

I can commit to:

- making a collage (Vision Board) on a sheet of paper of what I would like my future to look like;

  (Include things you are hopeful for. Incorporate all aspects of your life – family, diet, exercise, lifestyle. Pin the collage up somewhere prominent, for example, on a wall, wardrobe or mirror)

- using my board to encourage and inspire me to take one small step each day to create the future I see;

- considering when, where and how I can make my board a reality;

- maintaining my focus on enjoying the journey of life and having goals, however, not focusing on the outcome(s).

A simple story...

I experienced a very challenging season in my life and found it hard to stop thinking about what had happened. I let it define my confidence and I became fearful about my future.

These thoughts became still when I learnt to focus on the present moment and my breathing. Each evening I spent time just sitting quietly, breathing fully and taking note of the simple beauty all around me. I began to experience a level of peace I'd not felt in a very long time.

Challenge 2

Practise getting your thoughts to become still at least once a day. Focus on your breathing and think only about the present moment, what you can see and feel. Try to gradually extend the amount of time that you are able to do this for.

Rise above
my emotions

(Feeling)

Emotions can be a
response to a thought,
not necessarily reality.

Negative emotions
can arise from
repeated negative
thoughts.

53

My emotions are an indication of how I am feeling, however I don't always need to act on them.

My emotions and
feelings can change from
one day to the next.

My thoughts may try
to help ease emotions,
however they can
sometimes make things
worse because they
simply remind me of my
past or make me anxious
about the future.
This then gives my
emotions more energy.

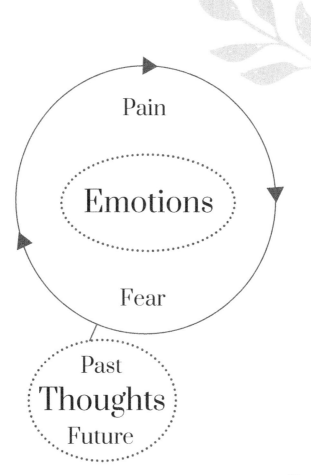

Pain

Emotions

Fear

Past
Thoughts
Future

My emotions are not who I am.

Keeping negative emotions inside of me can harm me.

Emotions such as jealousy and anger can feel really painful, but by letting go of these emotions, I am able to help myself.

People can only affect my emotions if I allow them to.

Considering my life more from a perspective of 'being' and one of love, can help me to have empathy, understanding and patience with others and myself.

No-one is
perfect and
we all make
mistakes.

Treating others as
I would like to be treated
is brave and forgiveness
is a choice, however
it's one I can benefit
greatly from.

I can
consider:

- writing down my thoughts if I am upset, angry or worried, to bring clarity and help me to put things into perspective;

- focusing my attention
  on the present moment and
  accepting how I feel, yet not
  reacting to it;

- surrendering to an emotion
  in a safe place in order to
  let it go if it is really intense,
  for example by crying;

- acknowledging that the
  negative feelings I have,
  are not who I am.

I can
commit
to:

- considering another way
  I could approach or look
  at a situation if I keep finding
  it stressful;

- being kind to myself
  if I feel overwhelmed,
  (for example: having an early night;
  taking a bath; laughing; taking time to
  do something I really enjoy; exercising;
  eating well)

- filling my mind with
  a type of food by:

  - watching, reading and
    listening to things that
    empower me;

  - spending time around
    people who inspire me.

A simple story...

I had experienced a physical pain in my body for 6 years that had not healed. I'd seen some of the best doctors and therapists I knew, however no-one had been able to help. After researching about the connection between physical and emotional pain, I felt that perhaps the pain might be caused from built up emotions I was carrying (resentment and unforgiveness linked to a past season in my life). I forgave and let go of these emotions and, remarkably, the pain went a way.

An inspiring quote:

" Love is patient and kind;
love does not envy or boast;
it is not arrogant or rude.
It does not insist on its own
way; it is not irritable or
resentful; it does not rejoice
at wrong doing, but rejoices
with the truth. Love bears
all things, believes all things,
hopes all things, endures
all things. "

1 Corinthians 13:4-7

The Bible: English Standard Version (ESV)

A scientific perspective:

When considering the influence of emotion on our well-being, we must first remember that our brains — where most of our feelings originate — are as much a part of our bodies as any other organ, fed by the same flow of blood, oxygen, and nutrients. Our emotions are linked to physiological reactions in our brains, releasing hormones and other powerful chemicals that, in turn, affect our physical health, which has an impact on our emotional state. It's all connected.

https://elemental.medium.com/how-your-negative-emotions-can-literally-make-you-sick-e6d8f363432a#:~:text=Our%20 emotions%20are%20linked%20to,a%20mind%20under%20 emotional%20stress.

Challenge 3

Consider replacing or minimising time spent watching the news, television and spending time on social media with reading, watching and listening to things that inspire and encourage you. Try also to make a conscious effort to spend time around people who have a positive outlook on life.

Use my words powerfully

(Speaking)

Speaking positively
will have a direct
influence on my future.

I have the ability
to alter the
direction of my life
just by changing
the way I speak.

I hear and use
my own voice and
words more than
anybody else's.

Therefore what I say
about myself and my
life is important.

The words that
I speak about
my life have
more impact
than anything
anyone can tell me
or say about me.

A scientific perspective:

A single word has the power to influence the expression of genes that regulate physical and emotional stress.

One negative word can increase the activity in our amygdala (the fear centre of the brain). This releases dozens of stress-producing hormones and neurotransmitters, which in turn interrupts our brain's functioning.

– Andrew Newberg, M.D. and Mark Robert Waldman,
Words Can Change Your Brain: 12 Conversation Strategies
to Build Trust, Resolve Conflict, and Increase Intimacy Paperback
– 26 June 2014

An inspiring quote:

"

Kind words are like honey–
sweet to the soul and healthy
for the body. "

Proverbs 16:24

The Bible: New Living Translation (NLT)

Speaking positive things daily is a way to increase my confidence and feel encouraged.

My words are powerful.

I can imagine my words like seeds. Good, kind, positive, encouraging things, will result in lots of delicious fruit trees.

Negative, unhelpful or
discouraging words can
result in things I don't want
to grow, like weeds.

My body, mind and emotions
react to how I speak.

I can consider:

- taking 3 deep breaths if there is something negative I urgently feel to say, to consider whether I really need to say it;

- having a good night's sleep before speaking negatively if I'm tired;

- facing facts, yet speaking with faith, hope and gratitude about life;

- expressing any complaint I may have directly and concisely with the person to whom it relates: Starting with a positive comment, not referencing past mistakes and ending with a suggested solution.

I can
commit
to:

- writing down and repeating 7 things (declarations) about myself that I am already, or that I aspire to be.

  (This doesn't have to be out loud. These words can be pinned up somewhere visible. Think about characteristics you would like to be able to use to describe yourself);

- being quiet sometimes if I don't have something positive or encouraging to say about a situation, person or myself or, phrasing my concern in a positive way.

A simple story...

I wanted to eat more salad and vegetables, however didn't like the taste of them at all, so much so, that the thought of eating certain ones would make me feel unwell. I began to tell myself over and over again, "I love salad and vegetables". Before long, my diet was completely transformed. Now, they are my favourite things to eat.

Challenge 4

Consider an area of your life or yourself where you'd most like to see encouraging change and make a conscious effort to speak positively about this area in every way you can, even when you don't feel like.

Be thankful & kind

(Giving)

Taking time to notice the simple, good things around me now can help me to feel positive.

(It could be as simple as being able to see, hear, walk. Appreciating the trees, birds, flowers).

The kindness I give
and the thankfulness
I speak of, sows a seed
for a harvest of kindness
and goodness to come
back to me.

Hard times
help me to grow,
develop strength
and resilience.
I can learn a lot
from them.

By helping someone who
maybe hurt or struggling
during challenging
seasons in my life,
I am able to shift the
focus off myself.

Yesterday has passed, there is nothing I can do about it, and tomorrow is not yet here.

It is possible to live joyfully, even though my life or things around me are not perfect or exactly how I would like them to be.

I can choose to
be thankful for
all I have in this
moment and
give from this
place too.

(Even if it's in a small way)

I can consider:

- feeling content and appreciating something about today;

  (Try to look around at some of the things you may see or experience everyday but sometimes take for granted)

- sharing the things I'm good at, enjoy or have experienced;

- learning as much as possible from a set-back and using it for inspiration.

I can commit to:

- doing something helpful and kind for someone each day;

  (It could be as simple as telling someone they look nice, sending a message of encouragement, or purposely smiling at a stranger)

- speaking about others in the way I would like to be spoken about, even though I may not always feel like it;

- treating other people in the way I would want to be treated.

A scientific perspective:

Expressing thanks may be one of the simplest ways to feel better. In positive psychology research, gratitude is strongly and consistently associated with greater happiness. Gratitude helps people feel more positive emotions, relish good experiences, improve their health, deal with adversity, and build strong relationships.

https://www.health.harvard.edu/mind-and-mood/in-praise-of-gratitude

An inspiring quote:

"Acknowledging the good
that you already have in
your life is the foundation
for all abundance. "

Eckhart Tolle

A New Earth: Awakening to Your Life's Purpose, 2005

A simple story...

For 15 years I had spent time most mornings running in one of the most beautiful parks in the city, however had rarely taken the time to appreciate the beauty all around me. I had been so busy focused on goals, a pace and times that I'd wanted to achieve that they'd consumed my attention. After a very long injury break, I returned to running with a deeper level of appreciation and I began to see for the first time, things I'd never even noticed. I felt lighter, faster and freer as a result of being thankful.

Challenge 5

Consider keeping a gratitude journal or simply just a piece of paper by your bedside to note down the things you are most thankful for each day.

Minimalise my materialism

(Prioritising)

My worth is not
related to my
life experience,
accomplishments
or anything I own.

There is nothing
that will make me
more valuable than
I am at this moment.

There is no need
to compare myself
to anyone.

Confidence and
greatness comes
when I embrace
what is within me.

I can take nothing
with me when I
leave this earth.

Taking a more minimal
approach to life can
help to bring space,
clarity and balance.

Being conscious about my lifestyle can help the planet and people who are affected by my choices.

Simple changes can make a difference.

I can
consider:

- de-cluttering my surroundings if I have an abundance of things, and giving some items to charity.

This can help someone else and can make you feel great too.

- how long materials take to break down if left in the environment.

  Wet wipes can take 100 years to biodegrade; styrofoam cups and plastic bags 500 years to forever.

- that there is little point in having the best and biggest material possessions if my well-being, and the people around me, have suffered as a result.

I can commit to:

- buying second-hand or vintage items;

- becoming more conscious about the amount of plastic and textiles I throw away.

- prioritising what is most important in my life;

- remembering that I am invaluable just as I am right now, and that a title, status or material things don't add to my true worth.

A scientific perspective:

Of the total fibre input used for clothing, 87 % is incinerated or disposed of in a landfill. Every year a half a million tons of plastic microfibres are dumped into the ocean, the equivalent of 50 billion plastic bottles. Microfibres cannot be extracted from the water and can spread throughout the food chain. Less than 1% of used clothing is recycled into new garments and every year some USD 500 billion in value is lost due to clothing that is barely worn, not donated, recycled, or ends up in a landfill.

Source: https://www.worldbank.org/en/news/
feature/2019/09/23/costo-moda-medio-ambiente

An inspiring quote:

" We ourselves feel
that what we are doing
is just a drop in the ocean.
But the ocean would be less
because of that missing drop. "

Mother Teresa

As quoted in Mother Teresa's Reaching Out In Love –
Stories told by Mother Teresa, Compiled and Edited
by Edward Le Joly and Jaya Chaliha, Barnes & Noble, 2002, p. 122

A simple story...

I simply wasn't aware that some of my lifestyle choices were affecting people around the world and the planet in such a major way until I watched a couple of documentaries. I was stunned to see the devastation to peoples lives as result of items I was purchasing and considered a 'bargain'. When I became conscious of this and the sheer volume of plastic used in my daily life (some things I did not even know contained plastic), I began shopping and consuming differently.

Challenge 6

Have a sort out of your wardrobe and consider giving items away to charity that you've not worn in a long time. You could even create a Capsule Wardrobe by mixing and matching a limited number of items of clothing and accessories. Assess your shopping habits to see if there are additional ways you could avoid using plastic, for example by refilling products as opposed to buying new containers.

Refuel & exercise purposefully

(Restoring)

Please note: If you do not have
the liberty of doing some or all of
the suggestions in this chapter,
that is OK! –Simply focus on the
things you can control.

With focus
I am able to
maintain an
effective and
enjoyable exercise
routine and eat
healthily.

Exercising does not
need to be expensive
or complex.

It does not even have
to be long. It does need
to be purposeful and
maintained.

(For example: Simply walk briskly for
20 mins, or jog and walk alternately
for 20 mins, or try skipping. Use
furniture in your living space for a
gym (stairs, chairs, the side of a bed
for squats, dips, step-ups; tin cans
for mini arm weights)

A scientific perspective:

Exercise is a powerful depression fighter for several reasons. Most importantly, it promotes all kinds of changes in the brain, including neural growth, reduced inflammation, and new activity patterns that promote feelings of calm and well-being. It also releases endorphins, powerful chemicals in your brain that energize your spirits and make you feel good.

https://www.helpguide.org/articles/healthy-living/the-mental-health-benefits-of-exercise.htm#:~:text=Regular%20exercise%20can%20have%20a,fanatic%20to%20reap%20the%20benefits.

An inspiring quote:

" Nothing will work
unless you do. "

Maya Angelou

@DrMayaAngelou, June 15, 2015

Eating simple, pure, natural foods (those with the least ingredients) are packed full of rich nutrients and will help me feel good.

(Check the labels on the foods you buy to see how many ingredients they contain. It's always good if you can understand what they all are!)

Hydrating well with water
throughout the day is key.

Getting adequate
sleep is a gift I can
give myself.

When I am fit and
healthy I have more
energy to give to others.

I can
consider:

- the direct correlation between sleep, diet and physical activity and my mental health;

- limiting refined sugar.

  (Other names for sugar include; fructose, sucrose, dextrose, glucose, maltose).

I can
commit
to:

- making regular exercise during the week a priority;

- giving my best effort to eliminate things from my diet which I know are not helping for me.

(Use Chapters 1–3 to help)

A simple story...

Desperate to change my diet
20 years ago as a result of
consistently feeling run-down,
I began experimenting with
eliminating certain foods from my
diet in hope to identify the cause.
Over time I found that a diet with
very limited refined sugar and no
dairy enabled my body to flourish.
As a result of creating a new diet,
based on alternative foods, my
energy levels improved and my
immune system was stronger.

Challenge 7

Consider if there are areas of your diet where you would like to see improvements. If you do consume more refined sugar than you would like, or you're constantly getting colds, providing it doesn't go against medical advice you've received, perhaps you could trial some alternative foods. For example, agave nectar as a sweetener instead of sugar, almond or coconut milk as opposed to cows milk (if you don't feel good after consuming dairy), to name just a few.

The only thing
that can stop me
from flourishing
is myself.

I can:

- breathe fully;
....
- quieten my mind;
....
- rise above my emotions;
....
- use my words powerfully;
....
- be kind and thankful;
....
- minimalise my materialism;
....
- exercise & refuel
  purposefully;
....
- live joyfully.
....